Internet Marketing

The Definitive Beginner's Guide

13 Proven Online Marketing
Strategies To Gain Tons Of Exposure
And Acquire More Customers

By Adam Richards

Table of Contents

Introduction

The role of Internet marketing in today's world is really far more impactful than you could ever imagine. Perhaps one of the biggest reasons that it is so popular out there today lies in the fact that it virtually costs 'nothing' as compared to other conventional means of marketing your product that have been around for years.

What's more, it's really a tried and tested methodology: it really works!

There are more people looking for products on the Internet today than ever before. But be warned: it's a literal 'jungle' out there in the fact that everyone seems to be doing it.

So why should you be doing the same thing, you ask?

Well perhaps for the very same reason a competitor

sets up shop next to one that is doing absolutely cracking business: because, quite simply put, that's where the customers are!

If you really wish to navigate your way through this vast digital jungle like a 'Rambo', you really need to take in account the several tried and tested strategies that will enable you to take your business a few notches higher than the others who might really seem to do the very same thing.

That's because there exist real 'methodologies' to penetrate the target market out there that until now have been available to only a select few. So let's take a look, then, in discovering just what they are so that we can take that business of ours to greater heights through astute planning. After all, the last thing that you would ever want would be to get lost in a jungle without a compass, wouldn't you?

Let it suffice to say that this book will serve to be just that: a compass to success!

Chapter 1:

Blogging

There's nothing quite like blogging when it comes to 'weaving a story' around that brand of yours.

Let's take a closer look at what it should entail.

Strategies for effective blogging for Internet Marketing

Make sure you define your target audience well.

Garnering a niche audience means that you will be catering to the needs of people who have a genuine interest in your product.

Make sure you present content with 'a twist'.

Your content should be fresh and original and in your very own 'voice' that will make it refreshingly different from other blogs out there. People are coming to you because they want something different. Make sure you give it to them.

Add content regularly.

A sure shot way for your target audience to lose interest in what you have to say is to keep long gaps between posting one blog and the next. Neither should you post too much and not be able to stick to it. Find a schedule that works and stick to it, say once a week.

Make a 'content plan'.

Every first week of the month, you might post something pertaining to industry tips. Stick to doing the same every month. People like the predictable.

Make sure that it is interactive.

Make sure that there is plenty of room for posting comments. People like to be involved. Give them a chance!

Keep it professional.

You really want to keep the look and overall design of your blog as professional looking as possible. Make sure that you do away with any spelling mistakes or grammatical errors that will only serve to make it look amateurish.

Make sure that it is SEO rich.

Use Google's Keyword research tool to find out which words and phrases are in demand. That can make all the difference in increasing the visibility of your blog.

Make sure it is optimized for social media as well.

Things like making it easy to retweet something you have posted by incorporating something like a widget, can really make a world of difference!

Pros and Cons of Blogging

Pros

Blogs are seamlessly integrated with search engine optimization. Make sure that it is integrated into your website domain for maximum results.

Online and print media sources look for blogs out there to get ideas for ideas on news and features. Guess where they will be looking?

It is a perfect way of providing that customer assistance especially if your product is far too technical and complex.

Cons

That content is 'forever'. Remember that once you post content out there you simply can't 'take it back'. Thus content that is defamatory or inaccurate or perhaps even confidential, can get you in heaps of trouble.

It is time consuming. It takes time to create that content that you post on a site. That time could have otherwise been spent doing something else of value.

Blogs need to include links to other sites. That means sending people away from your site. Do you want that?

Chapter 2:

Article Marketing

If you wish to be touted as an 'expert' in the realm of the product you are trying to sell, you might wish to give article marketing a most definitive shot!

Strategies for Article Marketing

Make sure that the content is relevant.

You could include pages that give various tips or suggestions about the niche that you are catering to. Or perhaps you could have pages that contain testimonials and reviews. But whatever you do, make sure that you have articles that are original and one hundred percent relevant to the niche that you are addressing.

Make sure that the keywords you use are relevant.

The potential users out there will be typing certain keywords in their browser to get relevant information pertaining to the product that they wish to buy, and by incorporating the same you ensure that your articles pop up higher than others in those search results.

Make sure that you backlink with those articles.

Whenever you post those articles on sites out there,

such as social media sites or perhaps even on blogs, you must ensure that you include backlinks to your company website so that the users who have stumbled upon your articles will be coerced into visiting your website and checking out your products, as well.

Use article submission services.

If you find the process of writing those articles to be too laborious and time consuming, then you might wish to employ the professional services of companies who will do the same for you albeit at a price. Certainly worth paying for the same where it comes to professionalism as far as enriching your articles with keywords and writing high quality articles is concerned.

Pros and Cons of Article Marketing

Pros

Almost all the websites out there that promote article marketing will allow you to insert that crucial

backlink to your company website.

Writing articles goes forth to establish you as an 'expert' in your field, thus making your product seem all the more plausible.

The links on those article directories are usually available for a very long time and thus provides a steady flow of traffic to your website.

Cons

It is not really all that 'easy' to write those articles. You need to have a real flair for writing and a lot of article directories out there have rather stringent editorial guidelines that you might not quite be able to bypass.

In the case of not writing those articles yourself, you might find that the process of hiring those ghostwriters for the same can be most expensive.

It can be most frustrating for you to continually find new ideas, especially if you have already written

several articles out there.

Those articles that you write will not generate a lot of comments. You don't quite know if it has gone down all that well with your audience or not.

This method of Internet marketing will work best for you only if you have stellar research skills and are a good writer. As discussed earlier it might not be all that worth it to hire a ghostwriter for the same.

14

Chapter 3:

Podcasting

Sometimes it's not quite enough to have text and other visuals; sometimes the power of the narrative is just what is needed to get your message loud and clear: hence, podcasts.

Strategies for Podcasting

 # Make sure that those titles are exciting.

This is something that the potential user first looks at. Make sure it packs a punch and whets his appetite to discover more.

 # Make sure the theme is applicable to a wide variety of people.

That's the best way you can ensure that it reaches a large number of potential users.

 # Make sure that you publish frequently over the first couple of months.

iTunes gives you 8 weeks to be featured in the 'New and Noteworthy' Section the day after you launch. Make sure that you make the most of it by posting at least three times a week.

 # Have guests promote you in their email lists.

That's a great way to tap into audiences that you

otherwise would not have gotten access to.

Get placed in those podcast directories.

Podcastland is an excellent example of the same. What's more, every month they let users vote for their favorite podcast and the user gets featured on their site for one whole month for free!

Create those sponsorship partnerships in exchange for free ad space.

You have nothing to lose here; all you have to do is mention those companies in your podcast. In exchange they can promote you on social media and any other channels that they would be open to promoting you on.

Tweet your episodes

Tweet episodes that are linked with SoundCloud so that they can be played within that Twitter Stream and reach more people.

Pros and Cons of Podcasting

Pros

They are easy to create. Those podcasts out there are really easy to create; all you need is a microphone or a standalone audio recorder with a USB cord and the appropriate audio editing computer software, and you are good to go! It's just a matter of a few minutes for those audio files to be edited; then they can be uploaded to your website or even to iTunes most easily.

The costs that are involved in the creation of a podcast are really minimal.

It allows a far better expression of emotions. Such things are not effectively conveyed in plain text form and besides, people like things being narrated to them rather than having to read them. It allows for a more personal enriching experience with the user out there.

Cons

\# They are not easily searchable. There is no major podcasting website for podcasts out there like there is 'YouTube' where video lovers are concerned. That makes it especially hard to search for podcasts. Even search engines do not help to a great extent. Besides, you can't merely skim through podcasts like you would in the case of print media to ascertain if it was something you wished to listen to.

\# Anyone can do it. This makes it all the more difficult for you to appear as a 'credible' source of knowledge as compared to several others out there doing the same thing!

Chapter 4:

Kindle Marketing

If you wish to capture the vast market out there on Amazon, all you need to do is capture the essence of your work ethos on Kindle and you are set to market your product out there. Of course it's not all that easy. Let's see just what it entails!

Strategies for Effective Kindle Marketing

Create a 0.99$ book offer via email.

You will be surprised at how effective this can be. Make sure that this promotion is over the course of a week and see the kind of visibility that you get in the Amazon marketplace. From then on you will find that Amazon will promote the book themselves on their various sales channels.

Incorporate that 'last chance' offer via email.

This is just before your book price is going to go from 0.99$ to 2.99$. This will serve as nothing short of a 'wake-up call' to those customers out there who will in all probability buy that book after all.

Venture with other authors

Be a part of a group author event where you will find that a few authors will cut their prices on their individual books as part of a joint campaign. The best part is that you will get exposure to their audience, as well!

Make sure that you use those 'Kindle Countdown Deals'.

These allow you to offer those books to readers for absolutely free for any five days in the ninety-day period. You will be amazed at the level of exposure this gives you. This can help generate that all-important traffic to your webpage and get your customers to know all about your company and product.

Include a link to your book in blog content.

That's a great way of getting more visibility out there for your brand.

The 'thank you' page.

When people subscribe to your list, they are brought to a 'thank you' page, which encourages them to check their inbox for that free offer and anything else that might serve to help your business.

Pros and Cons of Kindle Marketing

Pros

\# Amazon's on-site promotions are pretty spectacular and you could really be doing a lot for your business through Kindle marketing by getting the word spread out top a much wider audience.

Cons

\# Amazon provides you with no editing, proofreading and cover art. This means that your book will be published in the exact same manner that you submit it. It might appear a tad bit unprofessional to market your product doing the same if your work tends to have the touch of an amateur.

\# The submissions to Kindle are exclusive (in the KDP Select program you cannot submit anywhere else for 90 days) and that means that you might lose out in a big way to other markets where your work could have been published in order to drive the sales of your product. Amazon is the biggest player in the US and UK market but if your business is going to be catering to a global audience, then it might not be the ideal thing to do.

Just like in the case of 'blogging', if you have a penchant for words then this is the perfect way to promote that business of yours and take it to greater heights.

Chapter 5:

E-Mail Marketing

There's nothing quite as powerful as good old fashioned email when it comes to taking that Internet Marketing to an entirely different level.

Strategies for effective E Mail Marketing

Offers.

You need to make use of those marketing offers in your email lists in order for them to be really effective. This could be in the form of a discount coupon for some people who might be interested in a particular product or it could really be something of a promotional nature that is general to the entire target audience.

You need to build a strong value proposition that will be associated with the offer that you are trying to promote, though. You cannot look like you are merely trying to 'sell' something out there. You have to show you are helping the target audience in some way or the other by offering them what you have proposed.

Make sure that those email lists promote 'content'.

Your email lists must strive to educate people out

there with snazzy bits of information. There are two ways you could do this; by having links to content that are embedded within the body of the email or in the email itself. You could have opt-in forms that will allow the customers to share their personal data so that you can tailor content that is delivered to them based on their preferences.

Build those relationships.

By asking customers to fill in a survey or even replying to those emails, you can strive to foster a greater emotional connect with them, thus furthering your relationship with them.

Pros and Cons of Email Marketing

Pros

\# It is more cost effective. Working with contact information via email is faster and more cost-effective than gathering the mail addresses of people. There is no cost involved unlike in the case of traditional mail where the costs of printing and return postage are involved.

\# It is easier to track an email campaign rather than a standard mail campaign. You can track which emails were received and which were not; also find out who the people were who chose not to receive those emails from you.

Cons

\# It is really most possible for people to get a lot of marketing offers in their email boxes every day. They might just delete that email of yours before they even read it. What's more, the fact that you are in all probability using a bulk email program, will mean that you might just end up in the recipient's 'spam' folder, after all.

\# It might serve to taint your company's reputation. A lot of people out there are not in favor of unsolicited email and they might really be not too happy with the fact you are sending them the same. This might result in them thinking that your company is not all that reputable.

While there might be cons as far as email marketing is concerned as we have discussed above, it's a great way to market your product on the whole. That's because everyone really does check his or her email, after all!

Chapter 6:

Content Marketing

Content marketing is nothing but striving towards the same level of 'quality' that your product is all about. It's all about the 'relationship' you build with your customers over time.

Strategies for effective Content Marketing

 # Make sure that you have a dedicated team to manage that content well.

In the case of smaller companies, you might wish to have a single person who is responsible for the same. You have to understand that there needs to be a level of professionalism in managing content and it might help to hire a professional for the same.

 # Make sure that you create a wide array of content.

The last thing that you want is to become predictable. When you steer away from the tried and tested and create something that is refreshingly original, you actually strike a chord with your target audience in a way that you otherwise would never have.

 # Make a plan for up to at least six months.

The very fact that you have a plan in place for the

content that you are going to post, means that you will take the matter of posting most seriously and not succumb to not posting regularly, something that will only serve to hinder your content management strategy.

Make sure that you spend on that content plan.

It would be foolish to not spend on that content marketing strategy. You want to make sure that you allocate some of that budget that you have to that content marketing strategy of yours. After all, it 'is' one of the prime drivers of your business in today's age and you need to invest money as well as time in the same.

Pros and Cons of Content Marketing

Pros

It allows you to build a solid relationship with your customers. And the more interactive you are, you will find that your audience is more responsive. You need to understand that through the process of continually interacting with your audience, you really are in the process of creating sustainable relationships with them in the time to come.

It helps you glean valuable insights into the minds of your customers. It helps you understand them better and therefore enables you to strive towards the better fulfillment of their needs.

Cons

It requires a lot of time and commitment if you are doing it alone. If you do not have the funds to hire a content manager, you will see that it can be a most daunting task as far as the consistent creation of

exemplary content is concerned. Besides, you will have to do a lot of research as well, which is really not all that easy as it might sound.

It does not necessarily mean that there will be a call to action based on your marketing efforts. You might have written a great blog related to the product you are trying to sell, but you will find that not many sales ensue as a result.

In today's world it is critical for everyone to use content marketing to promote one's products. That's because most of the 'marketplace', after all, is 'online' these days.

Chapter 7:

Forum Marketing

Today's market is one that you cannot take all too lightly. People are informed and vastly educated and by harnessing the power of forum marketing to your advantage, you can work wonders in promoting your product!

Strategies for Forum Marketing

Choose the right forum for your niche.

You could ask your employees and customers about which online communities they hang out in. Or search forum hub sites such as 'Board Tracker' and 'Board Reader' using keywords that are specific to your niche, in order to determine exactly the right forum to post your commercial posts.

Create a great username.

Make sure that you choose a username that is easy to remember and to pronounce as well. Make sure that it is one that is understood by everyone, as well. The trick is to keep it simple while at the same time ensuring that the content that you post on your profile is compelling and articulate.

Make sure that that first forum post is intriguing.

You want to make people sit up and take notice of

you when you write that first post. Make sure that you don't look like you are merely trying to 'sell' your product and that you are here to significantly contribute to and learn from the community that you are now a part of.

Work effectively on the forum.

Find out how users interact on the forum and who the influential users are. Find out which are the hot topics and make sure that you back up any advice that you might have to offer with links to trusted sources. Make sure that you reply quickly to any responses you get.

Pros and Cons of Forum Marketing

Pros

You get to know the exact pulse of the market at any given point in time. You can find out what has people excited out there and work towards satisfying their desires. Or you can gain a unique understanding into their problems and then find ways in which you can strive to solve them.

By solving the problems of people out there, you will establish yourself as nothing short of being an 'expert' in the field and people will be all the more eager to buy your product in the future.

Cons

It takes time. And a considerable deal of it. Of course the dividends that you will reap from the process can be huge if you stick with it over the longest period of time. But in the beginning the process can seem very slow indeed.

You really do not know how people out there are going to react to what you have to say. There are all kinds of people out there and they will test newcomers in the beginning to find out if they are the right kind of people that they can benefit from.

It's really recommended for everyone out there in business to go in for forum marketing; this is a process that virtually allows you to get 'hands-on' experience while at the same time, remaining in the virtual word. It is truly the best possible way one can interact with their target audience.

Chapter 8:

Social Media Marketing

In today's fast paced digital world you will be losing out on a great deal if you don't consider the vast benefits social media marketing has to offer your product; it's really best to be 'social' in today's world, as you are about to find out!

Strategies for Social Media Marketing

 # Make sure that you treat each social networking channel as a separate entity.

You will find that in the case of LinkedIn, the target audience is one that will be most interested in 'clinical' businesslike data while in the case of Instagram, they will be looking for visually rich images that convey information.

This is particularly helpful to remember when conveying the same information through different channels; make sure that you keep it relevant to the demographics that pertain to the channel in question.

 # Make sure that you have a solid social media marketing plan and stick to it.

You need to know that you cannot have a plan that is constantly changing; make sure you have one that is most clearly defined.

Make sure that you use it most effectively as far as customer service is concerned.

This is the best possible platform to show your exemplary skills in customer service and by responding quickly to comments that are related to customer service and then actually taking action to back up the same, you will spearhead your social media marketing campaign towards the best possible results.

Make sure that you 'listen'.

You might feel like you 'know it all' when you establish your social presence online; the key to success, however, lies in listening to what your potential or existing customers have to say; that is the best possible way to ensure that you increase your market share over time.

Pros and Cons of Social Media Marketing

Pros

\# It is low cost. And that does not mean that you minimize on the 'reach' that you can achieve in the market out there; of course that doesn't mean that you do not wish to go in for an SMM (social media marketing) campaign strategy that is paid. Perhaps you could do that at a later stage.

\# It is fast. That's what you need, in order to get your products out there as soon as possible. You could even have your website synchronized with social media sites so that they can be updated whenever you have something new to offer.

\# It helps generate brand loyalty. The more personal interaction you have with your target audience, you will find that you strive towards creating a solid sense of brand loyalty with them.

Cons

It generates negative users. While it can be most instrumental in getting huge numbers of your target audience to gain interest in your product, it also attracts a host of spammers and scammers who only serve to harm your reputation online.

That ROI is hard to define. You might be investing a lot of time and effort in your SMM campaign, but the actual tangible results it brings might not be all that crystal clear to you.

No matter what, social media marketing is here to stay. One simply cannot imagine not using it for the furthering of one's business!

Chapter 9:

Video Marketing

This one's for people out there who like to make a 'visual' statement. This will work well to your advantage, if done properly. Let's have a look!

Strategies for effective Video Marketing

 # Produce a lot of content that is diverse in nature.

When you're posting on YouTube, you really wish to 'stand out' as far as the others doing it are concerned; and that means posting more videos about your product. Oh, and it helps to produce a wide 'range' of videos as well.

Besides them differing in nature, you want them to have varying lengths as well to provide an interesting mix!

 # Integrate that YouTube content with your website.

That's a great way to promote your product and gives your video campaign a greater degree of authenticity in the process.

 # Make sure that you engage with your audience on this platform.

This is a perfect platform to interact with people

who might be interested in using your product. Make sure you do just that.

Consider that YouTube advertising as well.

You do not wish to underestimate the power of YouTube advertising. It can ensure that you get up to ten times more of a click through rate than if you didn't opt for the same. It uses various hyper-targeting options to deliver the best possible results.

If you're looking to drive engagement and those calls to action, then you really do not wish to miss out on the benefits that this kind of advertising has to offer. It will help increase that 'sharing' of your video that will ultimately result in far greater views of your video in the time to come.

Pros and Cons of Video Marketing

Pros

The results are in real time. You can actually track the results of your video campaign on a minute-to-minute basis. You can even go to the extent of knowing where the person who is viewing your video is located.

It costs less. Of course this is one of the biggest pluses. It really doesn't cost anything to market your brand in the video world out there.

It has global reach. Anywhere in the world that people have a broadband connection, there is the opportunity afforded to them for that streaming video. Therefore you can literally reach every corner of the world through your video marketing campaign.

Cons

You can't force those people to view your videos. In all probability, people are going to wait for 5 seconds

and 'skip' that video ad of yours. The trick is in getting more people to really watch the whole thing and then share it. But then that can be very difficult indeed.

It's easy to book the wrong slot. You have to get that 'slot' right or else you will be catering to an audience that has no interest in what you are trying to say.

Your ads might appear on inappropriate content. Because the web is such a diverse place, there's really no way to ensure that something of the sort is prevented from happening altogether. That might lead to a most 'awkward' moment indeed.

Chapter 10:

PPC Advertising

You cannot underestimate the power of PPC advertising when it comes to the diligent marketing of your product. Using social media for promotion is one thing; using it to advertise is taking it to another level altogether.

Strategies for effective PPC advertising

Always include a call to action.

You really want to do this because you want something to come out of using this type of advertising, don't you? There should be some text or an image that suggests something like 'Click here for...' so that the customer viewing the ad is coerced to take things a step further rather than moving on to something else.

Targeting.

The targeting tool allows you to target your audience right down to the various countries that you want that ad of yours to appear in. Make sure that you make the best possible use of the same.

Make sure that your landing page is meticulously designed.

You don't want someone who clicks on your ad to arrive at a landing page that provides him or her with little clarity on what you are trying to offer them. Make sure that it is elaborately crafted and that it is easy to understand. You might wish to consider the use of graphics to make this page as visually appealing as possible and also have a subscription box so that you can collect their emails through the same.

Pros and cons of PPC advertising

Pros

It helps in the remarketing of the visitors to your website. It allows you the opportunity to convert them into leads or sales. After all, you don't expect someone to buy your product the very first time that they visit your website.

This helps you to reach out continually to them so that you really do stand a better chance at selling your brand to them.

It allows you to track ROI with conversion pixels.

Thanks to conversion pixels, it is easy to track ROI based on which keywords, ad messages and landing pages are converting.

\# It gives you really quick results. All you need to do is to create an account on Google AdWords or other equivalent channels. Next you have to bid on keywords that you think your potential customers will use while searching for products like yours.

Finally, you have to make sure that you point them to a specific landing page for optimum results and then sit back and wait for someone to click on your ad. It won't really be too long before you start seeing those sales results come in.

Cons

\# It can really be quite complicated. There are a lot of variables involved and if you do not have an effective strategy, then you might even end up losing money instead of making some.

It is not free. Of course, unlike SEO, it is not free and that's why a lot of people still choose the former when it comes to their online marketing promotional strategy.

The ads stop when your campaign ends. Simply put, once you stop paying, those ads disappear. That will mean that you will lose all that valuable traffic, as well.

Chapter 11:

Search Engine Marketing

The search engine is the biggest 'path' out there to scour the Internet for all the information you will need; here's a look at how we can make ourselves more visible than others on that magical path out there!

Strategies for effective Search Engine Marketing

 # Widen that horizon for niche friendly keywords.

Sure you're looking for those keywords out there; specific keywords that will give you the best possible results when it comes to that SEO strategy of yours, but you might wish to broaden the net a little for the best results.

You might even wish to target phrases that are commonly used. For example, if you are in the car rental business then something like 'Where can I get a cab in X' (X being the city you proffer your services in), can be most useful indeed.

 # Make sure that your website's URL structure is as uncomplicated as can possibly be.

You really want to make sure that there are consistent and search-engine friendly, as well. Broken links and errors will harm those search rankings. Also, pages with too many outbound links will also harm those search rankings as well.

Focus on fewer, 'better' links.

Those editorial links of yours should be solid; the ones that come from mentions of your company in the media out there. Also make sure you focus on those thought-leadership articles that you write for third-party sites.

To do that you have to make sure that you find a subject that is most interesting and not too promotional and then once you are done with writing, share it on social media out there. Ask to be listed alongside competitors in lists like 'The best players in X business' and make sure that you write copy that is aligned to the rest of that list in order to get there.

The Pros and Cons of Search Engine Marketing

Pros

\# It gives your company a real chance of solving that 'solution' out there. Most of your customers out there are looking online for a solution to their problems that your brand can solve.

This marketing strategy gives you sublime exposure to finding those very customers; or rather, having 'them' find you.

\# It generates traffic that has a real good chance at converting. Unlike in the case of social media marketing, the expectancy rate for people to be converted into buying your product is much higher in the case of search engine marketing.

\# A higher ranking sets you up as someone of 'authority' in your field. You will find that the higher you move up the rankings in the search engine results thanks to your stellar content, the higher this sense of 'authority' will be.

Cons

\# It has no guarantee for 'first page ranking'. Often, if you are not on the very first page of those search results, you will merely be 'ignored' by people out there who will only use the very first page for their needs. SEO marketing provides no guarantee that you will land up there.

\# It does not provide you full control. You do not know the kind of people you are going to attract and how much.

Chapter 12:

Press Release Marketing

If you're the kind of person that likes to make 'news', then this one's for you! Let's look at exactly what it takes to be an expert in the same field.

Strategies for effective Press Release Marketing

Optimize your press release.

You have to make sure that your press release is optimized with key phrases and links back to your website. In short, it should be search engine optimized. This will ensure that it will reach the top of those search engine lists quite quickly.

Do not write it yourself if you are inexperienced as a writer.

A press release must be as meticulously crafted as possible and therefore it is advisable that you hire the services of a professional writer, who will serve to keep it as professional as possible, if your writing skills are not to the tee.

Make sure that they are regular.

You need to be posting at least one press release every month if you want that press release campaign of yours to be as effective as can possibly be. If your organization has scope for posting more, then by all means post once every week. You will be amazed at the amount of buzz and thereby traffic you will be able to generate for your business, in the process of doing the same.

Use those website tracking tools.

These will serve to tell you how much of a spike there is in the traffic to your website on the day your press release is posted.

Integrate your press release with your marketing efforts.

There might be something 'big' that is taking place in your company, such as the launch f a new product or a certain deal that you are proposing to your customers. You might wish considering syncing that press release of yours with those events in order to reap the maximum possible benefit out of them.

Pros and Cons of Press Release Marketing

Pros

\# There are no advertising costs. It really is a great method of advertising that can be as effective as the other methods of advertising where you have to spend money in order to get your message through.

\# It sends out a stronger, more believable message. One of the best possible things about press releases is that they are far more believable than ads that look like they are merely trying to 'sell' you something. This can work wonders for your brand!

\# It has greater potential to spread. The media out there is always looking to find tiny bits of information that they can use; and press releases are exactly the kind of thing they are looking for. Who knows, yours just might make it to online publications out there without you having to even try!

It helps build your credibility in the media. Like in the point discussed above, the media might use your press release for their purposes.

Once you have seen that, you might wish to consider sending them your press releases yourself in the future. If they consider you credible, that might very well be the start of a most fruitful relationship with them in the time to come!

Cons

You need a really strong story. If not then in all probability the journalist out there will see straight through you and all your hopes of making it to the publication will be dashed.

You have to make sure that your story does not come across as another form of 'advertising', but that is really not going to be possible until you have a strong story, something that is not all that easy.

It takes a great deal of time and thought. It's really

not all that easy, even when you have a solid story that is needed as the above point would suggest, to effectively craft a press release that is worthy of publication. Therefore this can provide a strain on your resources in the ensuing process.

It's not 'direct sales', in the end. Even if you have a solid story and your press release has been crafted as elaborately as possible, it's not a given that it will end up in procuring those sales for your brand.

The message that is conveyed through press releases is very subtle, such as focusing on company integrity and the like, and it has to really impact the customer in a big way if they are to end up in buying your product, after all.

Chapter 13:

Online Classified Advert Marketing

If you wish to cater to a niche audience in the best possible manner, and gain that all powerful Internet presence as far as your business is concerned, then this one's for you!

Strategies for effective Online Classified Advert Marketing

Have a catchy title.

This might really seem all too simple but it is really the best possible thing you could do. Be most descriptive when it comes to the price and the key details of the product or service you are trying to offer.

Use keywords effectively.

Make sure that you use those keywords throughout the title and body of your ad. This is important because most people filter through keywords when looking for specific information; be choose to use the right ones.

Don't use heavy HTML coding.

Your post might end up being considered as spam if you do. Make sure that you keep it as simple and use only light coding wherever it is needed. Make use of text as much as you possibly can to convey your message effectively.

Post as often as you can.

While you might wish to post as often as possible for the best results, you do not wish to post too much. Posting more than once in a 48 hour window will only ensure that your ad is 'invisible' through a process called 'ghosting'.

Delete old ads.

When the 48-hour period discussed above has transpired, you are at liberty to post new ads that are similar to the old one. But make sure that you remove the old ad to avoid being flagged for removal.

Use Craigslist Ad Tracker.

This will help you to get an idea of which ads of yours are getting the most clicks. It offers a free and premium version as well.

Pros and Cons of Online Classified Advertising

Pros

It is absolutely free for anyone out there who has an email address.

As long as you are selling something that is 'legal', then it can be sold on Craigslist. There is a wide gamut of products out there that is being sold on the same, and thus you need not fit into a particular 'niche' in order to sell your products.

You can most effectively start an Internet based business, using Craigslist. The best part is that your email address is not visible to others if you choose to not show it to them.

Therefore, you can remain anonymous while successfully running a business from within the environs of your home itself!

Cons

You will not necessarily reach the kind of audience strength that you have in mind. This is because of the geographical manner in which Craigslist is segregated.

Therefore you will find that your advertisement is limited to the local area that you are selling in. Therefore if you are looking to reach a larger target audience then this can be a big hindrance. Of course one solution would entail rotating the ad in different geographical sectors, but that is a process that can be most time consuming indeed.

There is no valuable sense of protection that is provided to the seller out there as in the case of sites like eBay. Therefore, after you have made a sale you might find that someone writes you a bad check and you find it impossible to recover the money from him or her. In cases like this you have to rely heavily on trust.

Of course the plus side is that the advertising is totally free of cost, but you might find that you have a really heavy price to pay, in case of any losses that you might incur through the process of being scammed.

\# It might be really difficult if you are a newcomer to the site. This is because you will find that even for the slightest violation of the rules and regulations of Craigslist, you stand the very real risk of being spammed.

That means that you have to be extremely careful when posting on the site; you just might get bogged down by the excessive restrictiveness of the site where it comes to posting ads that will help your business grow.

Conclusion

Over the course of this book we have seen the thirteen different Internet marketing methods that you can use to make sure you take your business to an unprecedented level.

Each of these has been dissected carefully, allowing us to understand exactly what the most effective strategies are in case of each of the thirteen methods that we have discussed over the course of this book, and also the pros and cons that are associated in the case of using each method.

We have seen that there are some methods that differ significantly from others in the fact that they are most 'writing-sensitive' and a note has been made of the same.

You might consider using these methods on your very own if you have a flair for writing; perhaps you could hire a professional if your writing skills are not to the par but you think that these are the methods that you absolutely wish to swear by.

At the end one must realize that there is no magic formula for marketing one's product. For the most part one has to rely on their own sense of intuition where it comes to making a decision as to which marketing strategies are the best where it comes to promoting their product in the digital market out there.

Of course it is recommended that you do not merely stick to one; you really wish to make sure that you employ the strategies that you think form the perfect 'mix' where it comes to effectively promoting your product or service.

On the other hand, you really want to take on only as much as you can handle and not go overboard in selecting all the strategies discussed in this book merely because they all sound good.

So find the strategies that fit best with your sensibilities and intuition and go out there and conquer the digital world of marketing; watch those strategies help you acquire more customers and attract profits, making you every bit of the successful entrepreneur you always wanted to be!

I will be more than happy to learn how this book has helped you in some way. If you feel you have learned something or you think it offered you some value, please take a moment to leave an honest review on Amazon. It would help many future readers who will be forever grateful to you. As I will!

To Your Success,
Adam Richards

DISCLAIMER AND/OR LEGAL NOTICES: